ADDING LIFE TO YOUR YEARS

Adding
LIFE
to Your
Years

MARIAN BYRNE

VERITAS

Published 2015 by Veritas Publications
7–8 Lower Abbey Street, Dublin 1, Ireland
publications@veritas.ie
www.veritas.ie

ISBN 978 1 84730 632 6

10 9 8 7 6 5 4 3 2 1

A catalogue record for this book is available from the British Library.

Designed by Padraig McCormack, Veritas

Printed in the Republic of Ireland by Colorman (Ireland) Limited, Dublin.

Veritas books are printed on paper made from the wood pulp of managed forests. For every tree felled, at least one tree is planted, thereby renewing natural resources.

For my dad Gerry, who sadly passed away
before he could see this book finished.

Thank you Dad for a lifetime of love,
support and inspiration.

Contents

Introduction

As you start to read this introduction, I would love to be there with you to ask what prompted you to pick up this book. Perhaps it was something about the title or cover that resonated. Perhaps you flicked through it and some of the themes or headings appealed to you. Maybe it was recommended by a friend, family member or colleague. Whatever it was, thank you from me for following through on your instinct or curiosity.

One reason I would love to be there to ask is because the answer is important and a source of awareness. It can direct you to what you want to get from the book and the exercises along the way. Beginning with the end in mind helps with motivation, focus and success in anything. As such, it can be the difference between this being just another 'self-help' book, to be taken with a pinch of salt, to being a work that can have a profound influence on your life. So what do you want to get from it?

A second reason I would love to be there is because I am a coach who has worked with thousands of people for more than a decade and so have spent thousands of hours listening and asking questions, seeing what really works for people in practice (not just theory) and what makes a difference. I have been privileged to be part of their journey and have seen how they can change their thinking, their experiences and their lives.

The basis of coaching is twofold: it should be awareness-raising and action-oriented. Through the process, the person gains some new insight, perspective or clarity and is then prompted to take action which builds on that. The action moves it from information to transformation.

We are what we repeatedly do, as Aristotle claimed. He knew that so much of what we do and think every day is habit. Habit can work for us or against us, so consciously applying some of the information and exercises in this book for a set period can interrupt the old patterns or habits that are not to our benefit and introduce more useful and supportive ones.

The various sections and exercises are not just what I or current theorists recommend. They are what I have seen working for people to improve the quality of their lives. They have helped people to make the shift from just 'doing' to being. They are the skills that people have said really worked, that really made a difference, that were the turning point for helping them see how they could change their experience of life, regardless of what the circumstances of that life might be.

So while I am not claiming that this book will change your life, it can be the start of improving your experience of the one you have. It can help you to feel more positive or empowered, and the energy this brings can encourage you to embrace the bigger changes you want. It can be a starting point or a prompt, a reminder or a catalyst.

The most important thing you can bring to this process is openness: being open to a different way of thinking; being open to 'giving it a go'; being open to change. You will probably find there are some things contained in these pages that you do already, some you might start and continue to do and some that you feel are not for you. By being open to trying them though, you are finding what works for you from real experience and not from entrenched beliefs.

There are three themes that run through the book.

✦ **Self-Acceptance:** Acceptance of yourself exactly as you are is the starting point. From that perspective if there is something you want to change or add, it is positive and life-enhancing.

✦ **Awareness:** Increasing your awareness of yourself and others. Anthony de Mello maintained that what you are aware of you can control or change but what you are unaware of controls you. Sometimes the awareness itself can prompt change. Sometimes we have to consciously make a change in the way we think, what we do or how we are. Sometimes the awareness helps us feel more content or empowered because we now know that we are living life as we want to.

✦ **Movement:** This means moving from one perspective to another, shifting from theory to practice, freeing ourselves from being 'stuck' to getting started. It is a transition from negative to positive, a changing of focus from a 'reacting' mode to one of responding in a meaningful fashion.

You can use this book in many ways and I urge you to go with what feels best for you. This does not necessarily mean beginning with the exercise that seems easiest but rather starting with the one you think will make the most difference. So many of us pick up a book with initial enthusiasm but our attention drifts and often we don't finish it. Or we read on without actually doing the exercises or applying and integrating the understanding that may come from answering a question. In order to elevate this from being 'just another self-help book' to one that moves you towards change, think in terms of why it is that coaching works: it is about using the insight from what you have read and integrating it into your life by actively applying the insight and following through.

There are twenty-six sections in this book. If you focus on a section for two weeks at a time you will have completed them all over the course of a year. One suggestion would be to go through each in the order they are presented here. Pick a day and time to start and let that be the day and time each fortnight (or each week if you so choose) that you revisit it and then move to the next one. Take time to read through, reflect on and then think about how you want to apply it to your life or situation. Perhaps put a reminder of the theme in a prominent place (screensaver, bathroom mirror, fridge door, or just the book itself) so that it is a constant reminder of the fact that you are committed to change and improving the quality of your life.

Another suggestion would be to go through the book and pick a section randomly. The same then applies in working with the theme for the week or fortnight that follows. You may want to pick out the one that seems most relevant or necessary at that particular point in time for you. If you are doing it this way that's perfectly acceptable, but please also take the time to tackle the ones that may appear less appealing. They may be the ones you find most difficult or the ones that will provide the most challenges. Often the magic happens outside our comfort zone.

You may like to use the book with family, friends or a partner. This way you can support and encourage each other and hold each other accountable, as it were. You might like to chart your journey through the book in a journal, noting your initial reactions to an exercise, how you go about putting it into practice and what impact it has on your perspective. It can be a reminder of how we were feeling along the way and a way of recognising changes.

It can be easier to do something with help and support, challenge or a sense of accountability. As part of my journey with clients I have seen how we can start out well and then life gets in the way. We don't see results quickly enough so we put it down to an approach that 'doesn't work'. We feel down and wonder what the point is. We feel alone in it. But you are not alone. There are countless others who have walked and are walking the same journey as you. You are worth the effort it takes and the point is one made by several people before me: it is not about adding years to your life but life to your years.

Marian

Thank You

*He is a wise man who does not grieve for the things which
he has not, but rejoices for those which he has.*

Epictetus

'Thank you' – two little words that we often hear and use. We may
have been brought up to believe that they represent good manners
and respect. It's possible we have noticed that using them has a
positive impact. We can use them consciously or unconsciously.
Sometimes we may feel more grateful than others. But do you
realise that those two little words have the power to change your
life and the lives of those around you?

Saying 'thank you' is a way of feeling and expressing gratitude,
which is an emotion demonstrating appreciation for what we have
rather than what we do not have. The more we appreciate what is
good in our lives, the more of that good we attract and the better
we feel.

Gratitude is linked with increased energy, optimism and
empathy. It increases our sense of well-being and happiness. It feels
good. It improves relationships. It can be life changing.

✦ Take a moment and list five things you are grateful for in your life.

✦ Think of three people you are grateful to have in your life.

✦ Think of just one thing you are grateful for right at this moment.

How do you feel having done the above? Is your mood better than before you started?

Feeling good boosts our energy and positively impacts upon our physical, mental and emotional well-being. Gratitude is an emotion that leaves us feeling stronger.

Some people can naturally see the good in every situation and person. They are 'the glass-half-full' people who expect the best from life and who can turn challenges into opportunities, their biggest tormentor into a teacher and accept whatever comes with relative ease and grace. If you are like this, you are probably naturally grateful and appreciative of what you have in life. Your challenge may be in pushing through and knowing that it is okay to want more and have big dreams and goals, as well as being happy with what you have.

Others come into the world with a 'glass-half-empty' approach. They focus on what is missing. They focus on the challenges and seek people out who drive them mad at every turn! If you are in this camp, don't beat yourself up – just acknowledge that it is your particular way of looking at things and that you can change your perception of the same experience by starting to look for the positives or by being grateful. There are suggestions overleaf on how to discover what works for you. Some people say 'does that mean I have to do this stuff every day?' It may sound forced or impractical. However, consider how we approach personal nutrition and fitness – we form good habits because we know that it helps maintain our health and builds a positive self-image. It might be helpful to regard these exercises as being just as important in terms of our general well-being.

Exercises

So here are some suggestions for the weeks ahead. You can try one, some or all and find what resonates most for you.

✧ Each morning as you open your eyes, **be grateful** for the gift of entering a new day.

✧ **Keep objects of gratitude** – photos, stickers with quotes, etc. – in a prominent place so you can be reminded during the day.

✧ At the end of each day, **list three good things** that happened that day. This is something that you can also do as a family, group or couple. Share the three good things. At first you may have to reflect to find three things, but over time you will start to recognise and appreciate them as and when they happen.

✧ **Keep a gratitude diary or journal**. This can be in a journal or on your phone or computer. Having it written out and pinned up somewhere is also a brilliant way to keep the visual reinforcement and positive feelings that come with it.

- ✦ **Gratitude visit**. This is an exercise developed by Martin Seligman, co-founder of the field of positive psychology. Write a letter of thanks to someone who has had a positive influence on your life. If you visit them and read it to them it has the most impact, but posting it is a close second. It will have a powerful impact on you and them.

- ✦ **Write a 'thank you' note**. Taking the time to actually buy, write and post one is powerful, but depending on the situation or person you may text or email.

- ✦ Make a point of **saying 'thank you' consciously**. Take a second or so longer, look into the person's face or eyes and say it with meaning.

- ✦ **Look for the good in the situation**. When you have a difficult situation, ask yourself 'what can I learn from this?' Appreciate the learning opportunity and experience it brings to you.

- ✦ **Devil with the angel wings**. If there is someone you find very difficult, start by trying to understand what it is about them that is impacting negatively on you. What are they triggering in you? Thanking them (in your mind rather than out loud!) for raising your awareness and bringing that to your attention to resolve (either in yourself or with them) changes the impact they are having on you.

It can free you up to deal with the person and situation more effectively rather than feeling hijacked by the emotion.

These exercises reinforce the idea that no matter how bad we feel things are, there is always a lot to be grateful for. Even in very difficult or tragic times, people often reflect on how much support they've had; or, despite their pain, they acknowledge that they were able to get to a place of insight they may otherwise never have reached.

Role Model

All the world's a stage,
And all the men and women merely players;
They have their exits and entrances;
And one man in his time plays many parts,
His acts being seven ages.

As You Like It, William Shakespeare

A mother of four scanned the vacancies advertised in the local job centre. All the positions required experience. There were positions for a cook, a nurse, a counsellor and a financial adviser. 'Good,' she said, 'I can apply for them all.'

We all have different roles that we play. Along with our career role we may be a son or a daughter, a sister or brother, aunt or uncle, cousin, parent, spouse, partner or friend. In addition to these there are others that come into play: housekeeper, cook, gardener, student, volunteer, teacher, citizen.

Events and situations can lead us to take on roles. If you have a natural strength it may lead you to take on the role of organiser, helper or team leader. You may be the comedian in the group. The death or absence of a parent may mean you step into a central caretaking role for a short or lengthy period of time.

Each role represents different relationships and responsibilities. Each gives us the opportunity to be fully alive and engage with life, but as we grow and the number of roles increases it can put pressure on personal reserves. We can sometimes feel as though the roles are not of our choosing and that we have no control over them. This can lead to a lot of stress. We can expend great time and energy reacting to the demands of each role and lose ourselves in them while losing sight of time for ourselves. If we feel we have to be different in any one role (and pretend to be something we are not) it can be exhausting. If we are able to be ourselves in all the roles we play it takes less out of us.

We can also see how role quality and role quantity do not always equate. We can be present but *not present*: there in body but our mind is elsewhere – worrying, looking back or ruminating. If we are truly present, the quality of that time multiplies tenfold. Focus is increased and we will be more effective and productive in whatever role we are performing.

There are many and varied roles but the one that is most important, and often one we don't recognise, is that of just being ourselves with all the hopes, dreams and opportunities to experience life fully.

Exercises

A valuable exercise is to list the roles that you play in your life.

✦ What are your roles and what responsibilities are attached to each of them?

✦ Prioritise them in order of importance to you.

✦ Mark them in order of the amount of time they take each day.

✦ Mark them in order of the amount of energy they take.

✦ Which ones do you enjoy the most and why?

✦ Which do you find most challenging and why?

✦ What is working well for you?

✦ What changes would you like to make and why?

✦ What are you going to do straight away?

✦ What will take more time to change?

Pick your top three roles, in terms of priority, for the weeks ahead.

- ✦ Each evening, identify one exercise or action that you will do the following day towards fulfilling that role.

- ✦ No matter what happens or who is trying to get your attention, make sure that you do those three actions.

- ✦ By identifying the actual action in advance it will be easier to perform rather than if you have to come up with it on the day.

- ✦ By the end of each week you will have completed twenty-one exercises that will help strengthen the roles that are most important to you.

Remember that our relationship with ourselves is the first and most important one we have throughout life. We have both responsibility and the ability to respond. We need to choose the roles that suit us best and be ourselves in all of them. Life is too short to try to be anyone else.

First Thought of the Day

There are great primal thresholds in life, and one of the most beautiful and most encouraging and most healing is the threshold of dawn, when darkness gives way to the light and novelty and wonder of a new day.

Walking on the Pastures of Wonder,
John O'Donohue in Conversation with John Quinn

There is a song, popularised by Nina Simone, that goes: 'It's a new dawn, it's a new day ... and I'm feeling good'. Is this what you think first thing when you wake up in the morning? Do you jump up unprompted and feel refreshed or are you awoken in a state of agitation by the annoyingly familiar hum of your alarm? Even when we select a 'nice' alarm tone to wake us up it seems anything but when it actually goes off at 7 a.m.

What if that morning routine was one that we looked forward to? One that set an evenly balanced tone for the day ahead and that allowed us to be open to all the possibilities that the day can bring. Every day we have the opportunity to begin again anew. The first hour of the morning has been described as the 'rudder of the day' and so too are those first thoughts and moments.

A great way to start the day is to take time to identify what you want those first thoughts and moments to be. I have acted upon these helpful suggestions over the years:

✧ When you lift your head off the pillow you have all that you need.

✧ When you put your feet out on the ground you have the world at your feet.

✧ Today is a new day and the chance to begin again anew.

✧ Today I heal.

✧ Today, no matter what happens, I choose to love and accept myself exactly as I am.

Even if you find that the outside world 'comes in' all too quickly, by identifying what you want those first thoughts to be and then consciously bringing them to mind, you begin to break the vicious cycle where it seems that your thoughts are not your own. Even if in the beginning it is for a very short time, you focus on how you want things to be, rather than how you don't want them to be. You begin to be a deliberate creator in your own life.

You already have a routine for how you go about your morning. This has developed over the years. Perhaps you get out of bed and shower first, or breakfast first, or whatever it happens to be. Habit is good, as it allows us to do some things unconsciously so that we can use our conscious head space to focus on what is different or to be creative. Einstein had some of his best ideas when shaving and many people have come up with great solutions or creative ideas when showering. Sometimes, though, the habits may mean that we find life dull and repetitive. Changing things can create energy and also shake us up so that we initiate change for change's sake. This is like working the change muscle so that when we have to change in bigger ways, it's less daunting. Some simple examples might be to change the route we take to work each day or change the radio station we listen to so that we open ourselves to a different type of music, style of programme or point of view.

Exercises

Try to begin each day 'intentionally'. Be conscious of your normal morning routine.

✦ What are your first thoughts?

✦ How do you feel first thing in the morning?

✦ How do you want to feel?

✦ What do you want that first thought to be?

✦ How can you change your routine so that it will work for you and how you want to start your day?

The best wake-up call we can have is to know that when we are given a new day, a present, we can determine whether we want to live in it, or in the past or future. We can choose to set the tone for the day or we can allow circumstances, worries or others to do so for us.

Are Values Valuable?

Not everything that counts can be counted,
and not everything that can be counted counts.

Sign hanging in Einstein's office at
Princeton University

I remember my favourite teacher less for what I learned about the subject she taught me and more because she was the first person I could turn to for a sympathetic ear and a word of encouragement. She had qualities of empathy and kindness that were valued by a young secondary school student which are still important to me to this day.

We all have people in our lives that we love, respect and admire. We may not always be conscious of why it is that we hold these people in high esteem. So I want you to pause and consider a couple of questions. What qualities do you see in those you admire? What qualities would you yourself wish to demonstrate? Your answers to these questions will help you tap into your own inner values.

Values are what we believe to be important in the way we live and work. They can be the reason why we do or don't see eye to eye with someone. They can determine how we are in relationship, where we choose to live or holiday, which car we drive or whether we cycle, walk or choose public transport. We are normally uncomfortable with the idea of compromising our values.

We may view our moral code as a legacy from our parents and others who taught us values such as respect, honesty, integrity, tolerance or patience. We may admire in others characteristics such as creativity, a sense of adventure, courage, persistence, focus, confidence, discipline or fairness. We 'value' these things in other people and we may strive to be that way ourselves. When we feel we have not lived up to one of our own values, we can feel incongruent, inauthentic or uncomfortable. If we hold a particular value to be important we will feel annoyed when someone else fails to honour it.

It is helpful for us to try to uncover our values. When you think of a time when you were feeling happy, contented, authentic, it is likely that one or more of your values were being respected. You may have been with family or friends, been creative, or followed through on a challenge and felt immensely proud of yourself as a result. When you think of an occasion when you were uneasy or really angry or upset about something it is likely that one of your values was not being honoured. For example, it could have been a time you felt someone wasn't being honest with you when you wanted them to be upfront.

Your values will and should change and develop as you go through life. As we grow through our teenage years we will bring some of our parents' values with us, but should also develop and tap into our own. What is important to us through the teenage years and early adulthood may not sustain us through parenthood and the pressures of the workplace.

Sometimes we have to develop qualities hitherto untapped – such as focus and discipline – to help us achieve our goals. We may need to uncover courage and perseverance to help us cope with difficult situations. Many people look back at times of struggle and adversity as the times that built their character and helped them develop inner qualities that sustained them in life.

Sometimes we have to reprioritise. For example, financial security may be important for you, but if you embark on a new pursuit that values freedom, challenge or adventure, it may take a backseat for a time.

Decisions based on your most cherished values will always be more fulfilling. If you ever had a really difficult decision to make, the chances are there were two important values at play. If this were not the case, it would not have been so difficult to decide and you could have chosen freely. In a situation like that, understanding and naming the values at play makes it easier to see what you are choosing between. The benefit of identifying and reviewing your values is that you can understand why you do what you do and why others do what they do. This can lead to acceptance of oneself and others. Living according to your values is inherently fulfilling and satisfying.

Exercises

Take some time out to answer the questions below. Your answers will help you to clarify the values that are most important to you.

✦ What would you like to achieve in the intervening years between now and your next 'milestone' birthday?

✦ If you had to give someone three pieces of advice for living well, what would they be?

✦ What one or two words would you like people to use to describe you?

✦ Who are the people you love and respect and admire … and why?

✦ What moments do you relish?

✦ What are you most proud of?

✦ What are your best memories?

✦ What is your favourite quote?

✦ What legacy do you want to leave behind?

Values bring understanding to awareness, allowing us to live our lives purposefully – with purpose and for a purpose. They allow us to move from being a 'plaything of circumstance', a phrase coined by Viktor Frankl in his seminal book *Man's Search for Meaning*, to being the creator of our own experiences.

The Four Agreements

*Who stops us from being free? We blame the government,
we blame the weather, we blame our parents, we blame
religion and we blame God. Who really stops us from being
free? We stop ourselves.*

*The Four Agreements: A Practical
Guide to Personal Freedom,*
Don Miguel Ruiz

The Four Agreements is a book by Don Miguel Ruiz, published in 1997. For many, it is a life-changing work, whose ideas are derived from the ancient Toltec wisdom of the native people of southern Mexico. The Toltec were 'people of knowledge' – scientists and artists who created a society to explore and preserve the traditional spiritual knowledge and practices of their ancestors.

The four agreements are principles to practise in order to create love, happiness and peace in life. They focus on how we have self limiting beliefs that affect our lives and relationships. By adopting these four new agreements and challenging those beliefs we can transform our lives and those relationships.

Committing to these agreements is simple. Actually living them can be much harder!

Below is a short summary of the four agreements and how they can be powerful when deployed on a day-to-day basis.

1. Be impeccable with your word

The first agreement is the most important one and also the most difficult one to honour. It is so important that with just this first agreement you will be able to transcend to the level of existence I call heaven on earth. The first agreement is to be impeccable with your word. It sounds very simple, but it is very, very powerful.

Realise how powerful the words we use are, both when we speak about others and when we speak to ourselves in 'self-talk'. Often we are more negative towards ourselves than we might ever be to others.

'I am useless.'

'I am not as good, talented, clever, funny as …'

'I was so stupid to do/say that!'

What we think is our self-talk and what we repeatedly think we believe and become.

Speak with integrity. Say only what you mean. Avoid using your word to speak against yourself or to gossip about others. Use it to build ourselves and others up rather than bring us down.

2. Don't take anything personally

Nothing other people do is because of you. It is because of themselves.

Nothing others do is because of you. What others say and do is a projection of their own reality, their own beliefs. If we take things personally, we often 'shoot the messenger'.

Rather than hearing what is said, we may get defensive and two things can happen. We give out about the person who said it (who do they think they are?) or we take it all on board (it must be true if someone said it). If we do not take it personally, we can hear what is being said and ask ourselves 'is that true?' or 'might that be the case?'

If it is, we can take the feedback and use it in a constructive way.

If it is not, then we can recognise that it is their interpretation or projection and not be affected by it.

This agreement states that when you are immune to the opinions and actions of others, you won't be the victim of needless suffering.

3. Don't make assumptions

We have a tendency to make assumptions about everything. The problem with making assumptions is that we believe they are the truth. We could swear they are real. We make assumptions about what others are doing or thinking. We take it personally, then we blame them and react by sending emotional poison with our words. That is why when we make assumptions, we're asking for problems. We make an assumption, we misunderstand, we take it personally, and we end up creating a whole big drama for nothing.

Find the courage to ask questions and to express what you really want. Communicate with others as clearly as you can to avoid misunderstandings, sadness and drama.

If you would like help, ask for it rather than getting upset because no-one (or someone in particular) offered it.

If you notice yourself caught up thinking and replaying a situation or interaction in your head, stop and think: might you be assuming something that's creating discomfort or anguish? Someone passed you on the street and didn't say hello or acknowledge you. You may think they are ignoring you or upset with you over something. They may have been so busy caught up in the drama in their own head that they genuinely didn't see you!

Ask yourself empowering questions like 'is that true?' and at least explore the possibility that your reaction is based on assuming something – and it often is as we have to fill in the gaps to interpret things quickly. Once we realise that we are assuming something we cannot be as vehement about our original stance or interpretation.

With just this one agreement, you can completely transform your life.

4. Always do your best

Under any circumstance, always do your best, no more and no less. But keep in mind that your best is never going to be the same from one moment to the next. Everything is alive and changing all the time, so your best will sometimes be high quality, and other times it will not be as good.

Your best is going to change from moment to moment; it will be different when you are healthy as opposed to sick. It may be different on a Monday morning than it is on a Friday evening. If you know you have done your best, you can pick up and start again. Under any circumstance, simply do your best and you will avoid self-judgement, self-criticism and regret.

When we are experiencing a drama, it is usually our inner talk making assumptions which we then take personally. We beat ourselves up for not being good enough, perfect or right. Did you do your best? If so, what did you learn? What would you do differently next time? Resolve to do things differently, or look at what had an adverse impact if you have control over it (your energy levels for example) and do what you can to address it.

Exercises

If you notice you are stressed by something or someone just think which of the agreements might be of help.

Keep them visible so that you can reference them if you need to or as a reminder that keeps you on track.

In the beginning you will probably find that you have regularly reacted and made all sorts of assumptions, or taken something personally. On looking back and seeing which agreement would have helped, you raise your awareness of the triggers and of how you may be contributing to the drama. Over time you will develop an awareness as a situation happens and avoid the emotional rollercoaster that our 'faulty' thinking can create.

You may want to focus on just one agreement per day or week.

✦ Find out which one, based on your own temperament and difficulties, you 'need' most.

✦ Pick two or three positive affirmations which you feel are most needed right now. For instance:

'I make decisions easily and effortlessly.'

'I know instinctively what to do and say.'

'I am enough' … or … 'I am more than enough.'

'I connect easily and effortlessly with others.'

Saying and affirming one of those each day is much more beneficial and empowering than repeatedly stating the opposite.

Variety is the Spice of Life

Don't live the same year seventy-five times and call it a life.

Robin S. Sharma

Every cell in our body is constantly replacing itself. Biologists say that by the time you are finished reading a short sentence such as this, fifty million of your cells will have died and been replaced by others. We see a baby grow and develop in mind and body and, whilst less obvious on the surface, we know that there is continual development and change through life. PET and MRI scans can now show that whilst a lot of the groundwork or basic wiring is in place by the age of seven, there is a huge spurt of brain growth through the teenage years and into young adulthood. Neuroplasticity means that we can expand and develop our brains throughout life.

The seasons change and around us nature is constantly changing. Where water flows there is life. Where there is no flow there can be stagnation. Even as we stand or sit here the world is turning. The rate and scale of change in our daily lives is most obvious in the world of technology and in the amount of information available to us.

So we can see how life is about movement and change and expansion. Yet why do we so often resist change? Why would we cling to things as they are? Why would we cut ourselves off from fully experiencing life and all it can offer?

Some of the reasons include fear, confusion over what to do or how to do it, and a desire for the world to slow down; sometimes we lack patience or discipline through a process of change. It is linked to our natural temperament and our life experiences along the way.

So life is about having the ability to grow and develop and change. It is about expansion when we do, and stagnation and boredom when we don't. Even if we want to preserve a sense of safety within our comfort zones, after a period of time the comfort zone itself becomes uncomfortable. There may be nothing obviously wrong but we are not happy. We may feel that there is something missing. Addiction can often come into play as we try to fill the void with food or drink or consumerism.

If you are someone who naturally craves variety you may feel there is something wrong with you because you can't seem to settle for more than a few months or years at a time. This could be in a relationship, career or any facet of everyday life. You may be more sensitive to stagnation than others. Being aware of that and addressing it accordingly may help you to avoid sabotaging yourself in other ways.

Some people find that learning to 'practise spontaneity' can help. This might sound contradictory. However, if we are not naturally spontaneous, we have to consciously start to integrate it until it becomes a 'natural' habit. Spontaneity is important because it breaks routine and can generate a fresh perspective and energy. It is about living in the moment. In this context, I do not mean being rash or reckless but being open to change and to new experiences.

Tuning into and acting on your intuition is another helpful tool. Start to notice what your intuition is telling you and the outcomes when you do or do not follow it. That way you will recognise it and trust it which allows you to act spontaneously on it. So what forms might being spontaneous take?

✦ Leaving the pile of work on your desk to watch the sunset.

✦ Saying yes to the invitation!

✦ Booking the tickets when you notice yourself saying 'I would love to see that!'

✦ Taking a mini-break/time-out when it is needed, not when it is due.

✦ Striking up a conversation with a stranger.

✦ Having the dessert.

✦ Visiting a new place.

✦ Dancing the night away. As they say, no-one remembers the good night's sleep they had.

Exercises

Examine your daily routine and then seek ways to change it. Every day do at least two things differently than you would normally do. Some suggestions might be:

✦ Sit with someone else for lunch.

✦ Have something for breakfast, dinner or tea that you have not tried before.

✦ Have a bath instead of a shower or vice versa.

✦ Suggest an outing to family or friends (if you are normally someone who goes along with suggestions from others).

✦ Learn the basics of a new language (some great resources available now online or in app format).

✦ Change your hairstyle or appearance in some way.

✦ Read an article or watch a documentary on a topic that you do not know much about. This will not only help broaden our interests but may even offer new perspectives on some facets of our own lives.

✧ Go somewhere in your locality that you have not gone before. When we travel we often make a point of seeing and doing as much as we can but miss out on what is on our doorstep.

Change is natural and part of life. It is about continual growth and development. If something is not working as you would like then it makes sense to do something to bring about change. As Einstein famously said, insanity is doing the same thing over and over again and expecting different results. So exercise your change muscle, be spontaneous and seize the day!

Expert Advice

Advice is what we ask for when we already know the answer but wish we didn't.

Erica Jong

In his book *Outliers*, Malcolm Gladwell popularised Dr K. Anders Ericsson's theory that it takes ten thousand hours to become an expert in something: twenty hours a week for fifty weeks of the year for ten years. This theory has been challenged on the basis that it does not take into consideration how we learn or train.

The ten-thousand-hour rule should mean that each of us is an expert on ourselves! Yet we know that our level of awareness and cognitive skills determines whether we know and understand ourselves well or whether we have a limited view of ourselves that we just keep on reinforcing. We have certainly put in the hours but how well do we know ourselves, our motivators, our values and beliefs? Let today be the day to begin again and start to think and live in a way that acknowledges the person you are who is lovable and has potential. Let each day reinforce that belief rather than detract from it.

We often look to experts to tell us what we know we want to hear. It may be easier to hear it from someone else rather than accessing and listening to our own gut or inner wisdom. It may be that we find it hard to access our own advice. Take a moment to think of someone you know who is wise. What is it about them that inspires you? There is insight in that alone. When struggling to figure out what to do or how to deal with something, ask what might they do in this particular situation. If you can't think of anyone in particular, ask the question 'what would a wise person do in this situation?' The interesting thing is that when we ask ourselves that question we can usually answer it.

So what might stop us from trusting our own guidance? We might get it wrong! We might make a mistake! We have all gone through formal education which is exam focused and concerned with right and wrong answers. We come through it with a deep-seated concern for what is 'correct'. I saw a very apt phrase recently stating that mistakes are a bruise not a tattoo. Fear of making a mistake can lead to the really big mistake of not trying. If fear is preventing us from accessing our own intuition, we can ask 'what would I do if I wasn't afraid?'

We can only ever do our best and sometimes when we gain additional knowledge or take advice our best can become better so it is okay to heed what 'experts' may be saying. If you do listen to experts take advice that resonates. If something doesn't feel right it rarely is, so trust yourself rather than going along with something that might be right for someone else but not for you. You know yourself better than any expert and, regardless of how you feel you may have done in the past, let today be the start of trusting yourself.

It might seem implausible that there is a vast reservoir of knowledge and experience in each of us that can remain untapped for quite a long time. However, it is useful to think of times when we have listened to people with expertise in an area that we are familiar with – parenting for example – and notice the number of things that emerge which are truly new to us are probably relatively few. We might be surprised at the number of times the expert simply confirms what we already implicitly know.

Exercises

Imagine you are going on a radio programme as a guest expert on how to live life to the full.

✦ You give an overview as to why it is worth making the effort to do so.

✦ You highlight the consequences of not doing so.

Then the expert usually gives some top tips …

✦ What are your top tips for yourself on how to live the week ahead to the full?

✦ What advice do you have for yourself?

✦ What one thing will you start to do?

✦ What one thing will you stop doing?

✦ What are you already doing that is working well for you that you will continue?

Aristotle said that knowing yourself is true wisdom. Each section in this book can help you to know and understand yourself better and gain perspective on your life. Like all awareness we need to come to it with curiosity and acceptance and not judgement. From that point we can embrace what we have and adjust those facets of our life that will benefit from change.

Spring Clean

The more you have, the more you are occupied, the less you give. But the less you have, the more free you are.

Mother Teresa

Recently there have been quite a few reality TV programmes profiling the lives of compulsive hoarders. It goes without saying that the individuals featured are at the extreme end of the scale, with houses so stuffed with clutter that furniture is no longer visible; for the most part, the accumulated objects have no discernible value. Inevitably a decluttering team is on hand to offer assistance. Their hardest task is not clearing out the spaces but convincing the hoarders to part with any of the cherished throve. Although the shows are about 'major-league' hoarders they may still cause viewers to reflect on the baggage that they have accumulated over the years too.

A 'spring clean' can take place in spring, summer, autumn or winter. Take a few minutes to stop and look around your home. Is it as you want it to be? If someone came in and did not know who lived there, what might they say about the person who does? What clues are there as to your personality, style and lifestyle? Does it represent you as you want it to or is there a mismatch and why? Does it represent the 'you' you want to be?

If your environment represents how your mind works, what does it say about your interior life? If it represented your body and how you look after it, what would it suggest?

Allowing for the fact that you might live with someone or in someone else's space (spouse, partner, children, with your parents, housemates, etc.) think in terms of your room, wardrobe, car or even your office desk. Instead of throwing your hands in the air in despair, think in terms of what you have control over and have the ability to change.

This is about looking at your environment right now and taking control of the aspects of it you can change in order to make it as representative of you and your life as possible. By doing so you can create a space that's as supportive and replenishing as it can be. If it sounds like a great idea but too much hard work, or you don't know where to start, here are just a few reasons why it just might be worth the effort:

✦ Bringing order to disorder is empowering.

✦ If we feel stuck in one way or another, this is a great way of starting movement.

✦ As we move things on or around, we feel mentally, emotionally and even physically lighter.

✧ When our head feels clearer there is less anxiety and it frees us up to be more productive and creative.

✧ We save time looking for 'stuff'.

✧ We are less stressed trying to manage or move the clutter around.

✧ We can save money by not buying unnecessary objects.

✧ In clearing and decluttering we can identify and realise unhelpful shopping patterns we might have (whether that involves accumulating bags, coats, cushions or filling the kitchen cupboards with things that we end up throwing out because they are never or rarely used).

✧ It can give us the opportunity to start again or reinvent ourselves and let our clothes and environment represent the real 'us' here in this present moment.

# Exercises

If you are not yet convinced, perhaps start small over the week ahead and just try it out and see how it feels. Pick some small area of your life that is in need of decluttering.

It could be your car, desk, bag, wardrobe or cupboard. It could be a room or part of a room. Be ruthless – if you don't actually need it or love it, why is it there? What is the cost/benefit of keeping it or moving it on?

Be sure nothing goes to waste by following these tips:

- ✦ The motto 'reduce, reuse or recycle' is very helpful.

- ✦ Does a particular item need to be binned? Perhaps it can be passed on to friends, family, charity or sold on line.

- ✦ For items that don't fall into the above categories, put them into a bag or box with no label. Put them away and after a fixed period of time – it could be two weeks, two months or two seasons! – if you have not had to retrieve an item ask yourself if you really need to keep it?

- ✦ Another way of approaching it can be to take out all the items and only put back those you really need or love.

When you get a sense of the space and how that looks and feels only then go back with other items and see if they can now 'earn' their place back on the shelf or rail again.

✧ Take the seven-day challenge ... clear out seven bags in seven days.

How Rich Are You?

Money often costs too much.

Ralph Waldo Emerson

Research into the lives of lottery winners found that while their overall happiness level understandably rose when they won, after some months their happiness returned to similar levels as before their windfall. This prompted further research to explore the belief that money can't buy you happiness.

This research showed that when we spend money on other people, regardless of how much or the nature of the purchase, we feel happier than if we spent the same amount on ourselves. Buying a bunch of flowers to cheer someone up or treating a colleague to lunch has three effects: we feel good, the person who receives the gift feels good, and anyone who observes it feels good.

When we think in terms of 'riches' or 'wealth' we usually think in terms of money, assets, security. Many people spend a lot of time thinking or worrying about their financial situation. They invest a lot of time trying to generate income and look at how they can save time so that they can be more productive and generate more income or get some free time to enjoy life.

The relationship between time and money is interesting. A lady once observed that looking back over her adult life she either had lots of time and no money or lots of money and no time. It is interesting the way we think and talk about time. It seems intertwined with money in our minds and yet it is not a tangible commodity. The good news is that each and every one of us has exactly the same amount of time available to us on any given day. In that way there is absolute equality.

Our relationship with money is rooted in our past, our upbringing, experiences and values. We may view it as a measure of success or source of security. It may be a source of comfort or conflict. Regardless of the past or those bigger questions, we can look at two practical ways in which we can improve the quality of our lives and happiness. These are things we can do straight away regardless of our circumstances.

The first is looking at 'who' we spend our money on and the second is 'what' we spend it on. It is a given that we need to have our basic needs met. Food and shelter are basics. If, however, we are lucky enough to have some surplus beyond these, the other aspect to consider is what we spend our surplus on. Is it on experiences or things? There is research that suggests that we should consider investing first and foremost in experiences.

Whilst the experience often seems like a great option, many are swayed by spending on things. They represent tangible evidence of where the money went and may seem to have greater value. They do, however, start to depreciate after they are purchased. Wear and tear occurs, or perhaps the realisation that what we bought is not as essential as we first thought. On the other hand, if we spend on experiences, the memory becomes increasingly cherished with time.

By our nature and upbringing we will naturally be disposed to one or the other and you may well be thinking right now of an example that would prove the opposite of the above. The challenge is to just check it out for yourself: new couch versus French lessons; new TV versus weekend away; that pair of boots or jacket versus those concert tickets.

Exercises

In the weeks ahead look for opportunities to give either time or money to others.

✧ Take note of how you were feeling before, during and afterwards.

✧ What did you notice?

✧ If you are lucky enough to have surplus, notice what you are spending and where.

✧ Take a note of it as you go through each week (similar to a food diary!). This will allow you to be aware of how much and on what you are spending. If you are happy with your choices you will feel more in control and better about them.

✧ You may become aware of money that is being spent on things that bring you little or no physical or emotional return or which are of a very transient nature. There is no right or wrong here, just awareness of the cost versus return.

Finally, have a read through the quotes below and ask yourself:

✦ Which one resonates most with you?

✦ Would you like to change it or add to it?

✦ Which would be of most help to keep in mind in future?

Wealth is the ability to fully experience life.

Henry David Thoreau

Annual income twenty pounds, annual expenditure nineteen, nineteen and six, result happiness. Annual income twenty pounds, annual expenditure twenty pounds nought and six, result misery.

David Copperfield, Charles Dickens

Too many people spend money they haven't earned to buy things they don't want to impress people that they don't like.

Will Rogers

A wise person should have money in their head, but not in their heart.

Jonathan Swift

Wealth consists not in having great possessions, but in having few wants.

Epictetus

The greatness of a man is not in how much wealth he acquires, but in his integrity and his ability to affect those around him positively.

Bob Marley

Some things in life are priceless: good friends, health, nature, hope. For things that have a price, focusing on who you spend your money on can yield bigger returns on your investment!

Open Your Ears

We have two ears and one mouth so we can listen twice as much as we speak.

Epictetus

If I offered you a way to improve the quality of all your relationships, which involved no cost, therapy or lengthy training, would you be interested? If I told you it would also help you relax more, reduce stress and give you access to more information than you could ever ask for, would you be even more interested?

As Epictetus so rightly observed, we have two ears and one mouth so we should use them with respect to that proportion. What can often happen, however, is that we have so many opinions or stories to share, so much advice to pass on, so much to 'fix' that we do it the other way around. We let off steam, we talk *at* people rather than *to* them and often are not really listening because our mind is elsewhere or busy waiting to jump in.

Listening is the gateway through which we connect with others and get to know them. It is the best way to show someone respect and care and it helps them feel significant. When we really listen to someone they grow in confidence and self-esteem. This is true whether you are a parent, manager, colleague, neighbour or friend. It creates a connection whether it is with clients, family, friends or a significant other. We free ourselves of the pressure of 'fixing' or rescuing and get to realise that the person will often come around to the perfect solution or action themselves.

Over the past few years the number of people suffering from stress, depression, anxiety and loss has risen and one of the most important and effective supports is to be able to think and talk out loud. The Talk and Walk campaign advocates walking side by side which can make it easier to say what is on your mind rather than looking directly at someone or being in a confined space. Here, again, listening is invaluable.

You may be thinking that we all have to listen to get through the day. That is true but the way in which we listen and the quality of that listening differs.

Level one listening or 'surface listening' is when we are interacting with someone on an exchange basis. You tell me your story and I tell you mine. You say you had a bad day and I jump in immediately with 'me too!' and then go on to fill you in with the details of how bad it actually was. It is also called social listening as it can be on social occasions where the environment is not conducive to long or deeper conversations.

Level two listening or 'attentive listening' occurs when we are listening to the person and picking up on the non-verbal information too. Statistics vary slightly, but studies suggest 55 per cent of the impact of communication is body language, 38 per cent tone and 7 per cent the words we use. At this level we are listening more fully, but we may still have an internal dialogue about what we are hearing. We may be running the information we are receiving through our own filters and beliefs and conditioning. We may be judging what we are hearing through the prism of our own personal experience.

Level three listening or 'empathetic listening' is a way of listening and responding to the other person in a way that builds connection and trust. The Chinese character for 'to listen' is made up of the characters that mean 'eyes', 'ears', 'heart' and 'undivided attention'. This encapsulates the fact that listening as a whole body experience involves all of these things and is a powerful way to bring our attention and awareness to how we can listen well.

We listen with our eyes to pick up the non-verbal clues such as facial expression and body language. With our ears we hear the words and the tone used. We listen with our heart by being empathetic, not judging the other person or just hearing what they are saying but really understanding where they are coming from. We are completely focused on them in that moment and giving our undivided attention. We are not distracted by phones, what is going on around us or our own internal chatter. We are not just waiting to jump in with our story or opinion. We are really 'present'.

On a day-to-day basis we use level one and two regularly but how often do we allow ourselves to listen on that deeper, holistic, non-judgemental and non-directive way?

Exercises

On a practical level, look for opportunities to practise your listening skills in the week ahead.

On a day-to-day basis you will engage in a lot of **surface level** listening while interacting in a social or practical way. Paying for your shopping is a situation in which you usually interact on a surface level. If there isn't a queue behind you, take the time to ask a simple question in these situations and really listen to the answer. If we ask 'how is your day going?' and listen and comment on the response it takes the interaction from being a non-event to a moment of connection which could be the difference in the quality of that moment for them and you!

When you are listening **attentively** in a general sense, start to notice how much information you pick up from body language and tone. When we are on the phone, we tune in much more to the tone and pauses and breathing. This also accounts for the reason why there can be so much misinterpretation with written communication where it can be difficult to tell whether someone is being light-hearted or serious.

Notice if and when there is a mismatch. Feed back what you notice if it is appropriate to do so and you will be able to give that person some valuable information. For example:

✦ 'I notice that when you talk about x or y your face lights up.' Or 'I notice that every time you mention x or y you sigh'.

✦ Look for opportunities to listen emphatically with your eyes, ears, heart and undivided attention.

✦ If you find it hard not to 'jump' in with your own comments or perspective (old habits die hard) take a conscious breath every time you notice the urge to do so. Another technique is to put your tongue to the roof of your mouth while you are listening which makes it slightly harder to jump in. It is akin to trying to start a car in neutral.

✦ Notice how these conversations go. You will probably find that you will have an opinion or advice and don't offer it. The person usually reaches a conclusion themselves. It may not be quite the same conclusion as yours but they will feel more empowered if it is their own.

✦ Most of the time they will feel better having spoken about how they are feeling even if there is no obvious resolution at hand. Take some time to reflect on the following:

How did you feel during the conversation?

In what way was the outcome different from what you might have expected?

What did you learn about the other person?

What did you learn about yourself?

What impact did the interaction have on the relationship?

What might you do the same or differently next time?

If and when you need to talk, who are the people you can turn to who will listen and not judge or try to tell you what you should do? There will be times when you are looking for advice or for someone to offer a boost, but when you need a supportive ear you should have someone in reserve.

When we listen to someone it is the most powerful gift we can give both them and ourselves.

Cup and Saucer

Worry does not empty tomorrow of its sorrow. It empties today of its strength.

Corrie ten Boom

If you are a worrier there is a simple but powerful way of looking at life that helps you focus on what is needed and moves you from feeling powerless to empowered. Just think in terms of a cup and saucer. This is my way of explaining Stephen Covey's concept of focusing on what we can influence or change rather than what is outside of our control.

In his book *The Seven Habits of Highly Effective People,* Covey talks about our circle of concern and our circle of influence. There are a lot of things (and people) in and around our lives that concern or impact on us. Some people might be concerned about the way big business operates but have little influence in doing anything about it. Similarly, parents might be concerned about some of the choices their adult children make but are powerless to intervene.

Within that there is a smaller group of things which we have some control or influence over. We can actually do something about them. We can have a guiding hand in the lives of school-going children. We can influence the direction of local groups that we are involved in.

If, in any situation, we focus on something that concerns us but we cannot control or change, then we will experience a lot of frustration, anger or stress. We can swim around in these negative emotions but we are not actually able to do anything to change or influence the situation.

Often we feel we are doing something constructive merely because we are worrying or stressing over it, but we end up feeling worse and not improving the situation in any meaningful way. Continued worry and stress drag us down and leave us less able to respond to our own circumstances. If we focus on what we can influence or what we have control over, we are able to move beyond the stress and negativity.

In explaining this some years ago to someone who was finding it hard to grasp I used the cup and saucer analogy.

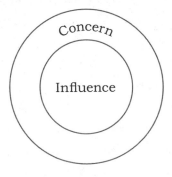

If you can, imagine the saucer as containing all the things which concern you but over which we have no control. The colour of our skin, the weather, the economy, the actions of other people and so forth.

The cup, by contrast, represents the things we can influence or control:

✦ Our own diet and fitness.

✦ Our own thinking.

✦ How we choose to respond to others. What usually happens is that we react to people and situations in very fixed ways. It takes awareness and a willingness to identify and choose an alternative response to implement positive change. A great example is the one-hundred and thirteen-year-old who was asked the secret of his longevity and he replied, 'When it rains, I let it'.

✦ The choices we are not making. For example, if we have a problem with someone we could choose to let them know they are bothering us but we may choose not to for a number of reasons. We may choose to reframe how we feel about them or look at our triggers (how they get to us). The key to choice is to be aware of what is happening and why. This will take away the hijacked feeling that can come when they press our buttons.

Exercises

Try this out over the weeks ahead. In any situation ask yourself:

Is this in the cup or on the saucer? Is it something I can do something about or not?

If it is not, look at what elements you have control over and think about how you will respond. The questions we ask ourselves determine how we feel and where our energy goes, whether on the problem itself or on finding a solution.

Some possible questions might be:

✧ What are my options?

✧ How can I reduce the impact this is having on me?

✧ How can I turn it around?

✧ Who can I talk to that may be able to help/listen/has been here before?

✧ What do I choose to do?

✧ What do I choose not to do?

When you move from focusing on the problem to what you can do, you move from fear and powerlessness to a sense of empowerment. You take control of your life and how you are responding to it.

Walking Tall

*Our bodies change our minds, and our minds can
change our behaviour, and our behaviour can change our
outcomes.*

Amy Cuddy

It has always been clear that our body language has a huge impact on how we are perceived, but does it have an impact on how we actually feel ourselves?

Work popularised by Amy Cuddy, Assistant Professor at Harvard Business School, on what is known as the Harvard Power Pose has recently been receiving a lot of attention.

In her study, volunteers did a 'power pose' (expansive, open body language) or a weak pose (closed in body language, chin down, ankles crossed) for just two minutes. Saliva samples were taken before and immediately afterwards and showed that for the power pose volunteers' testosterone (the hormone linked to power and dominance) increased by 20 per cent and cortisol (the stress hormone) had reduced by 25 per cent. This is consistent with increased confidence and a greater tolerance for risk or uncertainty. Those who did the weak poses, on the other hand, displayed the opposite results which are consistent with lower confidence. These two hormones are very sensitive to social and physical cues and fluctuate throughout the day in response to our body language.

Our body language, therefore, encompasses not just what is being communicated to others but what we are communicating to ourselves. Changing it changes our hormone levels, which influences our mind. This in turn can then change our behaviour, which can then change our outcomes.

In addition to the above, awareness of our body language and the link to our emotions is powerful. If we are feeling down or depressed, our body language reflects that and we tend to be hunched over with a downcast demeanour. This will not only change our internal chemistry but also makes it difficult to breathe as easily and effortlessly as we can when we are upright and more expansive.

To test this out, take a minute to think about something which you find sad or worrying. Allow yourself to tap into the thoughts that create the emotion. Begin to notice your body language. Now consciously stand up, tilt your head up and elevate your eyes slightly. Continue to try to think the same thoughts as before. What do you notice? People usually report that they either cannot fixate on the sad or dark thought as easily or that it does not seem quite so bad.

Now smile.

If you force yourself to smile, a real big toothy smile, your brain starts to think: 'Oh, they seem to be happy out there I will have to release some endorphins'. In an experiment two groups of students took a test and watched cartoons. In one group the participants had pens between their teeth to force a smile and the other group had the pen between their lips which forced a frown. The group with the forced smile found the test easier and the movie funnier than the other. The best way to prove this and reap the benefits is to try it out for yourself.

Exercise 1

During the weeks ahead, when you notice strong emotions, take note of your posture, body language and breathing. (It is easier at the start to catch the stronger emotions but pay heed to the subtler ones too.)

✦ What would others perceive based on your demeanor?

✦ Take a note of it if you can (mentally, on your phone or in a journal) and over the course of the week see if you can notice any patterns.

✦ What do the observations tell you?

✦ In terms of posture, what could you do differently? It is easier to identify an alternative when you are away from the situation so that if and when it happens again, you can employ that alternative rather than trying to come up with something on the spot.

✦ You may find at first that the situation has come and gone again before you thought of shifting your body default, but don't worry. If it is one of your default responses it will arise again!

✦ Obviously changing our thinking and shifting perspective are the most effective ways of changing our relationship with those thoughts over time, but for this week it is just about looking at how simple **physical changes can impact upon our thinking**.

✦ Smile when you don't feel like it; let your body dictate how you feel rather than your mind.

✦ Walk tall and hold your head up. Imagine there is a string coming up through the top of your head and it is gently pulling your head up. Allow your body to straighten and drop into a comfortable upright posture.

✦ Relax your shoulders (as they say in Pilates, many of us live with our shoulders as earrings!).

✦ Elevate your eyes slightly (where comfortable and safe to do so) and notice that there is a lot more to see up high than there is staring at our own navel or the ground.

Exercise 2

If you have an important interaction, meeting, interview or simply find the day ahead daunting, practise a few of the Harvard Power Poses.

✧ Stand tall and adapt an expansive open body posture (try putting your hands in the air or sitting with your feet up on a desk or table).

✧ Try the Wonder Woman pose (applies for men too so perhaps we will rename it the Wonder Person pose). Stand up tall and straight, feet slightly apart and hands on your hips with your arms and elbows pulled slightly backwards. No doubt the image of the actual Wonder Woman may come to mind and if that brings a smile … all the better.

Walk tall, smile and look the world right in the eye.

References

1. A. J. C. Cuddy, C. A. Wilmuth and D. R. Carney, *The Benefit of Power Posing Before a High Stakes Social Evaluation*, Harvard Business School Working Paper, No. 13-027, September 2012.

2. F. Strack, F. F. Martin and L. Stepper, *Inhibiting and Facilitating Conditions of the Human Smile: A Non-Obtrusive Test of the Facial Feedback Hypothesis*, J. Pers. Soc. Psychol., 1988, May; 54(5): 768–77.

Coming to Your Senses

Lose your mind and come to your senses.

Fritz Perls

We have five senses and at any given moment we are using at least one or more of them. Even as we sleep our senses continue to gather information from the world around us. Our brains have nothing else to go on except the information delivered by our senses. In this context, the term 'to come to your senses' means to tune in to what our senses are telling us, to think sensibly.

When we are feeling really stressed our bodies go into one of three of the 'f' modes: fight, flight or freeze. One of the best ways to turn off and stop the stressful thoughts from spiralling is to 'come to our senses'.

Tapping into our senses takes the focus away from thoughts and brings us right into the body and into the moment. Right now, close your eyes for a moment and become aware of:

✦ Anything you can hear …

✦ Anything you can smell …

✦ What you can touch …

✦ What you can taste …

When you have finished, open your eyes and, without adjusting your position or moving your head, become conscious of what you can see. Look at it as if you are seeing it for the first time.

It is the simplest way of challenging our standard response and taking back control of what is happening.

On an ongoing basis, you can become more aware of which sense has the most impact for you and can build up an environment which is 'sensory rich' in a way that works for you. You can have what you need with you so that you can tap into it whenever you need to. For example, if you are a visual person, having objects, photos or images that calm or lift your spirits will help. Know what colours you find soothing or uplifting and use them in your environment or incorporate them into what you wear.

If you are heartened by sounds, have music or aural stimuli that you can tap into if and when required. When music affects our brainwaves, it also affects bodily functions. Our breathing can slow down, our heart rate drops and it can activate the relaxation response and reduce cortisol.

For the other senses it works in a similar way. If smell is key for you then think of aromas that would enhance your environment – perfumes, aromatherapy oils, flowers, fresh tea or coffee, sea air, etc. If touch is central for you, then a soft blanket or scarf may be ways of honouring this preference. Similarly, you can respect your partiality for taste by mindfully and slowly eating or drinking something.

If we live and work in an artificial environment, our senses are not being naturally stimulated on a daily basis. Schools, colleges, offices and many of our communal spaces have recycled air and glass to keep out the elements (but these also keep out the natural sounds). We live in a world of polished surfaces and clothes made of man-made materials. Colours are often kept neutral. Food is mass produced or processed so we miss out on the amazing flavours of organic produce.

We miss out on the stimulation of our senses, the quality it can add to our experience of daily life, and the brain growth it can encourage. Our senses work to engage our attention and make the brain more alert. Using two of our senses increases the likelihood that we will remember something, with smell being the most powerful sense for memory. That explains why the smell of cut grass brings us right back to our childhood. A perfume or aftershave can reminds us of someone significant in our lives. The aroma of home baking, coffee, flowers, the sea or the pages of a new book can contain a feast for our senses.

The second reason that embracing our senses is invaluable is that it leads us to be more mindful of the world around us. These days there is a lot of focus on awareness and mindfulness as an antidote to our stressful lives and to help achieve inner peace. Awareness and mindfulness are, in essence, paying attention. Where do you put *your* attention?

Exercises

Below are some steps that you can take to build up the habit of paying attention. First, identify an activity that you can commit to doing mindfully. It could be your morning wash or shower, cleaning your teeth, preparing food, or walking.

✧ Each time you engage in the activity, bring all your attention to what you are doing.

✧ Do it slowly and consciously, engaging all the senses.

✧ Any time you notice your attention wandering or the busy mind trying to sabotage your few minutes of mindfulness, come to your senses …

✧ At the start of the week you may find it difficult to keep in the present and keep the focus on the task at hand. When this happens just smile (don't beat yourself up!) and come back to the present.

✧ As the week goes by just look for examples of progress by taking note of the number of times your mind tries to take over or the length of time you do the activity for.

✧ By the end of the week reflect on the experience. This is a form of meditation that everyone can do.

If you think you don't have the time to 'slow' down the experience or to waste good thinking (stressing) time, then that is a definite sign you really need to do it. In this case, doubling the number of tasks you do consciously is highly recommended.

Story of My Life

There are no rules in filmmaking. Only sins. And the cardinal sin is dullness.

Frank Capra

If your life was a book or a film what type would it be? Adventure, romance, comedy, fantasy, action, thriller, horror or tragedy?

What would you like it to be? How would you describe yourself in the leading or star role? Do the people around you see the real you or are you wearing a mask? Are you playing the part as you think it should be played or how you think others think it should be? Would the movie engage you? What emotion would you be feeling if you were watching or reading about the character and the story so far?

If we step back and think of our lives in terms of a story or adventure, it allows us to observe past events objectively. It gives perspective and invites us to take control and realise we have more power in the creation of our life experience and direction than we had thought.

One interesting way of doing it might be thinking in terms of *The Hero's Journey*, a book by Joseph Campbell, an American mythologist, writer and lecturer. His work is often remembered or summarised by the words, 'follow your bliss'.

The title of his book, *The Hero with a Thousand Faces*, reflects his concept that all hero stories, consciously or not, follow the same pattern of the ancient myths and journeys. There are thousands of stories, myths and legends but within them all there is really just one story. There are three 'acts' or parts – separation from the ordinary world, initiation and return – and each has a number of individual stages which cover the typical journey.

Act One

✦ Living in our ordinary world.

✦ Call to adventure (this is usually when we are challenged, a time of change or when we are forced to 'go out' into the world in some way).

✦ Refusal of the call (we are stuck, there is fear).

✦ Meeting of a mentor (someone who helps us to start the journey).

✦ Crossing the threshold.

Act Two

+ Tests, allies, enemies.

+ Approach the innermost cave (getting to the point where we no longer want to live the way we were living. We can take no more. We are tested to the limit).

+ Supreme ordeal (the defining moment, event or period of time when we face our fear. The biggest crisis. The darkest day. The breakdown before the breakthrough).

+ Seizing of the sword reward (taking power into our own hands, the death of fear. We realise we were fighting ourselves. We are so immensely proud of what we have done or achieved).

+ The road back (how do we integrate this new learning and confidence and peace? We might think we need to 'stay' where we are to continue feeling how we feel and be reluctant to return to where we started).

Act Three

✧ Resurrection

✧ Return with the elixir (the final piece is to be able to live in the moment. To live without fear. To share this new you, knowledge or power with your community. The journey was yours but the benefits can be shared).

Campbell's work inspired George Lucas' approach to the *Star Wars* movies, and the same journey can be seen in *The Lion King*, *The Wizard of Oz*, *Superman*, *Rocky* and many more. The hero's journey can inspire us to go beyond the limits we set ourselves, to face adversity and allow our inner resources carry us through, to live life to the full and know that everything that happens is part of our journey.

Can you think of a time in the past when you have been on this journey?

Are you at a stage in the journey right now?

If you view your life overall, would thinking in those terms help you reframe your experience of your life?

Exercises

So step into the writer's or director's chair now. You have artistic licence for the next part but begin with the end in mind.

✦ What way do you want this to end?

✦ What story do you want your life to tell?

✦ What does the lead character need to do?

✦ What other characters need to be introduced, removed or kept on in the plot?

✦ What would you be most proud of? Remember that this is the story of your life. It is not for a general audience so you are not trying to please everyone. It is for you alone so you can write it as you want.

Find an image or quote that represents what you want to achieve and how you want to live. Keep it in a prominent place. Look at it regularly.

✦ What one thing do you need to start doing right now?

✦ What one thing do you need to stop doing?

✦ What one thing are you going to continue that is working perfectly?

Joseph Campbell himself said that most people were not seeking the meaning of life as much as the experience of being alive. From today you can start to consciously be the leading character in your own life story and decide how you want to play it from here on out.

Less Stress, More Success

Less Stress, More Success is the excellent title of a series of exam revision books. Less stress not only allows us to do and achieve more, it is also good for mental, emotional and physical wellbeing.

So what is stress? If you Google that question you will get a mind boggling number of 'answers' which only serve to leave us more stressed trying to understand what it is! There is no one answer. It will be different things for different people and our perception of what stress is and how it affects us is just as important as the 'stress' itself!

One of the definitions which I did find most useful is this:

> *Stress is the perceived imbalance between the demands being made on us and our perceived ability to cope.*

Some key words in that definition are at the heart of understanding stress.

✧ Perceived refers to *our* perception but not to *everyone's* perception. We view (or perceive) the world through our own individual lens built on beliefs, values, past experiences, self-esteem, self-awareness and thinking skills.

✦ Imbalance suggests that there is a mismatch. The demands are more than what we think we can deal with.

✦ Demands being made on us are predicated on the degree to which we feel we have control over the person or situation. Something is often stressful to the extent that we feel we have no choice or control.

Essentially, stress can manifest itself by our desire for things to be different, and not feeling we have the skills, choice and control to deal with the situation.

A certain amount of stress is essential to help us grow, test our boundaries or take us out of our comfort zone, helping us to reach our potential. All of the above means that stress is our reaction to the triggers in our lives. This is different from saying that the triggers themselves are the source of the stress. You may be thinking, 'that can't be so – what about financial concerns, moving house, illness or working with a tyrannical boss?' They certainly are challenging but if you think some more about it you will probably be able to identify someone who does not seem to worry about money as much as you do, or seems to be able to take that difficult boss in their stride.

So how can we focus on taking back some control and choosing how we want to offset some of the more day-to-day stresses we encounter?

Exercises

Think of a daily situation or event that causes you stress. It might be your commute, an overflowing email inbox, or your ever expanding 'to do' list. Take a moment to think through what exactly it is that causes you stress. Pick an example of a day and go through the sequence of events as they happen.

✦ What are you doing at each stage?

✦ What are you thinking?

✦ What are you feeling?

✦ What is going on in your body?

✦ What could you do differently?

There are some very simple techniques to decrease stress on the following pages. Pick one or two and try them out in the week ahead to reframe those everyday stressors.

Breathe

Imagine a grid and breathe in for the count of four as you 'walk' up the left side of the grid, hold for four along the top, breathe out for four as you go down the right side and rest for four along the bottom.

+ Breathe deeply into your stomach area rather than your chest, noticing how it rises and falls like that of a baby. Infants know instinctively the best way is to 'belly' breathe, but over the years we lose sight of that perfect rhythm.

+ By visualising the square you block out internal noise and can focus on breathing correctly.

+ If you find it hard to hold for a count of four, you can do it for three to start and build it up to four or five.

+ As you breathe in, hold and breathe out slowly. The 'rest' at the end is a moment of pure stillness and calm.

+ Just doing a few rounds of this square breathing regulates your heartbeat into a lovely rhythm. It also leaves you in an optimal condition if you have to face something like an exam, a presentation or a difficult conversation.

Think and talk out loud

✦ Externalising something often helps to shift our thinking around it. Often, we don't need anyone to provide insight (in fact it is usually better if they don't!) but we get perspective and relief by talking it through.

✦ Talking 'shoulder to shoulder' is non-threatening and supportive and safe.

Focus on the solution not the problem

You need to explore the problem or stressor to identify what is at play, but then spend your time and energy on the solution to the problem. Ask yourself:

✦ What can I do?

✦ What are my options?

✦ Who can I talk to?

✦ How can I turn this around?

✦ How can I reduce the impact it is having on me?

✦ How can I turn this into an opportunity?

✦ What have I learned from this?

✦ What do I choose to do?

Three 'A's

Ask for help, allow people to help and accept help when offered. This might sound very simple but some of us are so busy helping everyone else we find it hard to ask for help for fear of seeming weak. 'I don't want to feel obliged' or 'they might not do it the way I want it done' or 'it is a sign I am not coping'. Whatever the block, if you are feeling stressed or overwhelmed try this simple but powerful technique.

✧ You get help and reduce stress.

✧ Those helping get to feel good. If you are good at giving you know how it feels. If you do not accept help you are depriving someone of that opportunity.

✧ The world operates as it should in that we are all connected and are here for each other. There are over seven billion people in the world and they are here for a reason.

Each day life will offer us opportunities to stress if we take up the offer. Choose instead to take the opportunity to try some of the above and any other techniques that you come across. Choose to engage with life rather than resist it. Choose a new response.

References

1. Irish Lifecoach Ltd training manual.

Don't Sweat the Small Stuff

Don't sweat the small stuff, and it's all small stuff.

Quote and title of book by Richard Carlson

Enjoy the little things, for one day you may look back and realise they were the big things.

Richard Brault

Above are two quotes that seem to contradict each other. But if we reflect on both we will learn two lessons about the small stuff, recognise where it stands in our order of priorities and enjoy it. Both prompt us to be aware, to understand what is important and what is not and to keep things into perspective.

Only you can decide what is small stuff and what is not. If you are house proud you may have a tendency to spend a lot of time keeping your home in order but face the challenge of ensuring that doing so does not come at the expense of sitting down and talking or connecting with your loved ones. If the pressure to have things perfect leaves you stressed out you might have to accept that a little clutter in the grand scheme of things is a small price to pay for a happy household. Conversely, for others mess and clutter may be contributing to anxiety and may not be a small matter at all.

Only you can identify what is most important in your circumstances. Does the way you live your life demonstrate what you regard as important and what is less important? If we do not reflect on our priorities we can easily fall into the situation of giving attention to things that really do not mean a lot to us. When you figure out what matters most it is much easier to make concessions in other less important areas.

Exercises

What are the moments you cherish and why? What can you do on a daily or weekly basis to create more opportunities for the things you are passionate about in your life?

Who or what are you taking for granted? How can you change that?

Who or what are you giving too much time and attention to? How can you change that?

Thinking back over the past two or three weeks, can you identify some 'small stuff' that you sweated over? Knowing what you now know, how can you avoid doing the same again?

Think of some issue that is preoccupying you at the moment and ask yourself if this is something that is going to continue to occupy your time and attention.

✦ Will it matter in three weeks, three months or three years from now?

✦ If it will matter over the longer term, do what you need to do. It helps you to realise that what you are doing today is an important piece of the jigsaw.

✧ If not, then do what you need to do let it go.

The key to a good life is this: if you're not going to talk about something during the last hour of your life, then don't make it a top priority during your lifetime.

Don't Sweat The Small Stuff, Richard Carlson

Mindfulness

Breathing in, there is only the present moment.
Breathing out, it is a wonderful moment.

Thích Nhất Hạnh

Who among us would not wish to be less caught up in our minds? Less stressed by the constant conversations we have with ourselves in our heads? Less reactive or hijacked by emotions? Who wouldn't want to be able to feel calmer, more centred or in tune?

Many people find that practising mindfulness is one way of helping to achieve that equilibrium. Being mindful is about bringing your attention in a non-judgemental way to your thoughts, emotions and experiences on a moment-to-moment basis. It means:

✤ being more aware of and connecting with your body.

✤ being more aware of your mind and thought patterns.

✤ being aware of your emotions.

✤ managing your reactions so that you can respond accordingly and not reacting in a way to triggers that may be unhelpful.

It is about gently observing your mind and body moment by moment. The following exercises give a little flavour of what is meant by this non-judgemental awareness; it does not try to achieve or change anything but to make us fully present in the here and now.

Exercises

Square breathing

✦ Sitting or standing in an upright position, take a few seconds to become aware of your feet on the ground and your connection with the earth below.

✦ If it is possible and you feel comfortable doing so, close or lower your eyes.

✦ Bring your attention to your breathing, your own natural pattern.

✦ What do you notice? Don't judge or try to interpret anything, just notice.

✦ Then visualise a grid and use it as a structure to breathe in an even and regular way. To start, use a count of three or four but as you practise this more you may feel comfortable to breathe for a count of five or six. The key factor is that it feels natural and not strained in any way.

✦ Visualise breathing in as you 'walk' up the left-hand side of the grid for a count of three and then hold across the top for three, then breathe out for three and then pause along the bottom for three.

✦ Repeat this exercise several times and then just allow your breathing to return to normal.

✦ Become aware again of the connection of your feet to the ground, and in your own time you can open your eyes.

✦ How do you feel afterwards?

✦ What, if anything, is different?

✦ The purpose of using the square is to give a mental image to distract us from our thoughts, keep our breathing in check so when we breathe in and hold and then breathe out we are actually focused. That pause along the end is pure stillness.

✦ The added bonus is that when we breathe in this way our heartbeat will slow and we will find ourselves in an optimal state in terms of focus and creativity.

✦ Obviously this is something you can do at any stage of the day without having to close your eyes, but for the first few times it is more powerful to do it that way so you can really highlight the impact it can have.

Eating mindfully

✦ This is exactly what it suggests. Eating in a mindful way involves being fully present and conscious of what we are eating by relishing each bite or spoonful, noticing the flavours, the texture and chewing our food thoroughly. Take your time and savour each bite, avoiding distractions such as your phone or watch.

✦ Eating mindfully takes us out of our head, allowing us to fully appreciate the food that is keeping us alive and nourishing us. It is a natural way of regulating how much we eat because it prevents scoffing. We notice how we are reacting to the quality and quantity of what we are putting into our body. It can allow us to feel grateful for having the food. It may highlight how much we are missing or perhaps taking for granted.

✦ Pick one meal or snack a day to begin. Start by doing this at the weekend or a time of the day when you are less rushed. The more you practise it, the more you will appreciate how powerful it is and this will motivate you to make it a regular fixture in your daily routine.

Walking mindfully

✧ How often do we go for a walk only to use the time to continue performing mental gymnastics? There are times when walking allows us to explore an idea or get clarity on something, but often we go for a walk to clear our head only to find that we bring our problems with us.

✧ Walking mindfully is a way of getting out of our heads and reconnecting with ourselves and our surroundings.

✧ At a very basic level if you find your head is so busy that the thoughts keep coming in – and you can't imagine them like clouds passing by as is so often suggested – then bring your attention to your steps or strides. Think right, left, right, left, right, left. This will distract you from a 'busy' head.

✧ Notice the feeling or impact as each foot connects with the ground.

✧ Look around you. Notice what or who you can see. Don't judge or assess or get involved … just notice. If you are walking in nature (which is ideal but not always possible) really connect with your surroundings. What can you smell? What can you hear?

✧ Every time you find that you are back in your head, just redirect your attention to your surroundings or movements.

Mindfulness is awareness, which is attention. Where is your attention? You may think you can't tackle your distractions but if you are not directing your attention, then who is? Practising mindful awareness helps you realise that we have more control than we might believe.

Making Memories

I will use memories but I will not allow memories to use me.

Deepak Chopra

Jean-Dominique Bauby, in his inspiring memoir *The Diving Bell and the Butterfly*, recounted how, despite being completely paralysed by a catastrophic stroke, he was, thanks to the power of memory, able to fly like a butterfly from the room where he lay and revisit his past.

We all live in the present. However, we have this great mind that can rewind and go back or fast forward and try to predict and plan for the future.

Memory develops in the womb and is there to enable us survive, learn and grow. It enables us to form connections and relationships. It allows us to get through the day smoothly. Like our bodies it needs to be exercised to develop or maintain it through life.

Lack of sleep and stress can impact memory function. When people are under long term or intense short-term stress they often find that they forget simple things on a regular basis. Dealing with the cause of that stress will not only improve your quality of life and physical health but free up your memory as well.

Memory allows us to look back on lovely past events and enjoy the warm feelings they invoke. However, we often use it in a way that is not useful or empowering. How often do we go back over a row or situation that upset us? We relive it over and over again. Think of a movie that you really hated. Would you take it out every day and watch it on repeat? If you did just think of the impact that would have on how you feel.

Yet we may repeatedly relive something 'bad' we have done. Feeling guilty or ruminating about it may, perversely, make us feel better. Learning from what you did (which of my own values did I undermine?) or seeing what action you can take to address it are positive ways to move on. Replaying the memory, for its own sake, keeps us rooted to the past and has no benefit.

If we have had a row with someone we may replay it in our head and get repeatedly indignant or upset, keeping us fixated on the negative. Think, in this instance, what needs to be done and what needs to be discarded?

Remember also that our memory can be faulty! Memory is the process by which we acquire, encode and then store information which we retain and can later recall. There may well be a scramble between what we see, hear or experience in acquiring the information, and what we actually record or 'encode' in our mind and memory.

If I meet someone who tells me their telephone number and am distracted at the time, my thought process is disrupted and I am more likely to enter the information incorrectly. It is then stored the way I recorded it at the time.

Our memory may be distorted in a similar way and so is not always reliable. We can record our perception of what happened rather than the 'reality' of it. That is why two people in the same situation (and depending on their own temperament, beliefs and experience) often have two completely different memories of it.

Exercises

Moving memories on

Think of a memory that you are comfortable recalling, but which you may think is not a 'good' one.

✧ What were the events that occurred at the time (think in terms of a neutral observer recounting it)?

✧ What were your actions in response at the time?

✧ What were your emotions around it?

✧ What are your thoughts and emotions about it now?

✧ What might that neutral observer say?

✧ Is there anything you would do or say differently if that was to happen again?

✧ What is important for you to take from it for future reference?

✧ How do you feel about it now?

✧ Is there anything you want or need to do to allow you to free yourself from the influence of this memory?

✦ What can you do to change it from being a negative one to an instructive one?

Conversely, how often do we take out the good memories and replay them? It is certainly very important to do that if they are helping us feel good, empowered or connected.

List some of your key 'best memories' …

✦ Are there any common denominators?

✦ This is giving you great clues and feedback as to your values and what you may want more of in your life.

✦ To what extent are they in your life at the moment?

✦ What can you do today to start the process of re-introducing them?

Making memories

Looking to the month or year ahead, list down the experiences you would like to have. Not just the 'to do' list but the 'to feel' and 'to be' as well.

✦ Think big, medium and small. It could be walking on a beach at sunset, watching a film outdoors, climbing a mountain, being kissed by someone who thinks you are wonderful, surprising someone, surprising yourself, telling those you love that you love them more often … make your list!

✧ If you approach each day from the perspective that you are making memories, you notice and enjoy the moment more and chances are you will not waste time on things that are not worth remembering.

Use today, the present, to consciously make your memories for the future … don't use it as an opportunity to rehash ones that you don't want from the past.

Judgement Day

Love is the absence of judgement.

Dalai Lama

People who have experience of conducting interviews with job applicants often report that they make up their minds about individual candidates in about the time it takes for that candidate to be seated in front of the panel. How can they make up their minds so fast? Obviously it has nothing to do with what the prospective employee has said. There hasn't even been a chance to say anything! It seems that the important things are to do with body language, posture and eye contact.

Whether we like it or not, we are programmed to judge. We do it to ourselves and others on a daily basis. Judgement and being judgemental are not the same. We need to make judgements each day to evaluate all manner of things, from the amount of time a task is going to take to what we feel is right or wrong in a given situation.

Being judgemental, on the other hand, is finding fault with the behaviour, beliefs or decisions of someone else based solely on personal opinion. We don't just observe but make judgements based on assumptions and on our own beliefs and opinions. Often we don't question our own bias. When we judge someone else we are not defining them but ourselves.

More often than not we can be our own worst critics too. We can judge ourselves against unrealistically high standards. We generalise and criticise. We say things to ourselves that we would never dream of saying to a friend, a child or partner. We tell ourselves how stupid we have been. Think how you would feel if someone spoke to a loved one in such a condemnatory way. Of course you would want them to be encouraged rather than to be judged or criticised.

The most important thing we can do for ourselves is to love and accept ourselves exactly as we are. It is the basis of happiness, hope and health. From that place we can set goals and look for change if we want, but if we do not like ourselves as we are then day-to-day life will feel like an uphill struggle. The less we love and accept ourselves the steeper the hill and the harder the struggle.

Exercises

Being judgemental of oneself

1. Notice your self-talk. Is it negative and critical?

2. If so, interrupt the criticism and pause it.

3. Evaluate it. Does it propel you to action? The chances are good that it sabotages that action.

4. Use good judgement to assess your next move – one that allows you to show love and compassion to yourself.

Being judgemental of others

The process is the exact same – notice, interrupt, evaluate, be compassionate.

The opposite of being judgemental is loving and accepting ourselves and others exactly as we are. We have peace in the present, and with a clear head and heart use our good judgement to know what we need to do to reach our potential in our lives and our relationships.

Music to My Ears

Music produces a kind of pleasure which human nature cannot do without.

The Book of Rites, Confucius

Since the early 1990s 'The Mozart Effect' has been popularised among parents, promoting the theory that listening to classical music would make children smarter. A healthy market in classical music for children was generated as parents hoped some of the genius of Mozart, Beethoven and others would rub off. Whatever the merits of those claims, there is endless evidence of the importance of music to our development from the very start of our lives. Parents sing lullabies, children often sing rhymes. Hearing complex music, such as classical compositions, develops the same pathways in our brains that we use for mathematics, so from the very start it helps our brains develop in ways that may seem unconnected.

Music also connects *us*. We meet people through dancing, going to concerts, playing music and singing along together. Think of the start of a national sporting event with people standing shoulder to shoulder singing their national or sporting anthem. We can travel the world and music is a common language. It is often used to mark life events from birthdays and weddings to funerals. It can bring us back in an instant to the time or place when the piece was originally heard, evoking memories of a cherished person or event.

Music can bring us up when we are feeling down, relax us when we are stressed, inspire, motivate and move us into action – just think of what you might listen to if going for a walk, run or having a workout.

Exercises

Whether music is something that you have been consciously incorporating into your life or not, a challenge for you is to:

✧ Go back and listen to a song or piece of music you love but have not heard for a while.

✧ Listen to some live music – a concert, a busker, a local band – whatever you are most drawn to.

✧ Dance – around the kitchen or bedroom on your own or take a dance class. When you do, dance like no-one is watching.

✧ Discover a 'new to you' artist. Listen to some music that you have never explored before. If you love classical music, find a contemporary artist or vice versa if you have a preference for pop.

✧ Make playlists for yourself; music to relax or chill out to. Music to get you up and going. Music to soothe the soul or inspire.

✧ Think back over your life and put together a musical timeline or playlist of music that is significant for you and which punctuates your life. It could start with the song that was number one on the day you were born, or the theme music to some of your favourite childhood TV programmes; perhaps a favourite song that someone sang for you, or the first piece of music you bought or danced to, the piece of music or song which you would like as a theme song for your life.

In doing any or all of the above you are rewiring your brain, recharging your body and re-energising your life. If music is part of your day and your life and you love it, then well and good. If not, be open to accessing an invaluable resource that is readily available in many forms and allow it to enrich your life.

Vent

Anger is just anger. It isn't good. It isn't bad. It just is. What you do with it is what matters. It's like anything else. You can use it to build or to destroy. You just have to make the choice.

White Night, Jim Butcher

In workshops to explore conflict and anger, a facilitator I know used to ask a volunteer to stand in the middle of the room and say to other participants, 'If that person is conflict, where in the room would you be? Think about that and take up your position'. Some would walk right up to 'Conflict' while others would get as far away as possible, in some cases leaving the room.

We tend to think of conflict and anger as negative or something to be avoided. Anger can make us feel bad, or makes us do and say things that we regret. It can eat away at us in a most destructive way. We have all witnessed or experienced the consequences of it. So people tend to try and mask it, redirect it or suppress it.

However, every emotion we have serves a purpose. It is there to draw our attention to something. It is saying look at this, look at me. It is giving us an insight into our values and thinking. If we ignore what it is trying to tell us we miss an important insight or opportunity.

Anger as an emotion is there to tell us that our boundaries are being broken, that our values are in conflict or that we are really passionate about something or someone. If you allow anger to hijack you it may worsen the situation. If you ignore it, you will have to ignore your inner guidance system and long term that can lead to illness, depression or lack of self-esteem.

✦ Learn to recognise the signs that you are angry.

✦ Press pause and take a step back: breathe, go for a walk or a run or talk to a friend.

✦ Identify what it is about.

✦ What value or boundary or belief is being challenged?

✦ Are you making any assumptions or taking something personally which is not personal?

✦ How might you be contributing to the situation?

✦ Does something need to be said or done, or do you need to take a step back, accept or reframe the situation?

Passive vs assertive vs aggressive

Thinking about the differences between being passive, assertive or aggressive can be illuminating when dealing with the emotion of anger. Passive means that my needs are not as important as yours. I defer or put you first. I don't speak up. Aggressive means that my needs are more important than yours. It's all about me and I have no problem speaking about them. Assertive means equality is present and that both views are important. We may confuse assertive with aggressive, and if we know someone who has a very strong aggressive style it can stop us from speaking up as we do not want to be like that person. If we are passive we may 'put up and shut up' until one day we eventually erupt. Think in terms of assertive and use that as your guide.

Saying yes and saying no

Start to notice when you say yes and no. Are you saying yes because you want to or because you are afraid to say no? If I say yes to this, what am I saying no to? If it is not a yes that feels right then trust your intuition and be assertive by saying no.

Get physical

If we are really angry there is a physical response as well as an emotional one. The old cartoon depiction of getting angry involved steam coming out of a character's ears, while he or she turns crimson with rage. Whilst the scientific explanation may be more accurate – heart rate up, testosterone levels up, cortisol levels down – we can all observe in ourselves and others that physical response.

So by working our bodies we can release some of that tension by going for a walk or a run, punching a cushion or pillow or doing some very intense housework. Alternatively, gardening brings us in contact with the earth and that literally does have a grounding effect.

Exercises

Write a letter to someone expressing what you are angry about. Read it later that day or the following day and notice your reaction to what you have written.

✧ Ask yourself, have your feelings changed? Do you need to do or say something?

✧ If so, having taken time to reflect, you can now be more effective in what you do or say.

✧ If not, is it time to move on?

✧ Either way burn or bin the letter … it was never meant to be sent but to help you honour your feelings in a constructive way.

Use anger as a prompt to action. Be mindful however that the action may be within yourself. Or to help you find a way to let it out safely rather than allowing it build internally and then erupt. Respond rather than react.

Nine Things that Can Help or Hinder You

Obstacles don't have to stop you. If you run into a wall,
don't turn around and give up. Figure out how to climb it,
go through it or work around it.

Michael Jordan

A learner driver in the UK failed the theory test one hundred and ten times and spent almost five thousand euro in the process. This would-be driver is not alone in needing multiple attempts to reach a goal, but while such persistence is admirable it begs the question: is there something wrong with the method of preparation?

When we are stuck it does not feel good. We often beat ourselves up for not doing something, but that is usually because we are in the middle of a situation or are so close to it that we have lost perspective. Einstein once said that the significant problems that we face today cannot be solved by the same level of thinking we were engaged in when we created them. In other words, if you keep doing what you are doing, you keep getting what you are getting; if nothing changes, nothing changes.

Below is a tool taken from Michael Neill's book *You Can Have What You Want* where he explores the things that can hold you back or help you to move forward. He calls it the 'Obstacle Analysis Grid'. It is a quick way of separating the nine major categories of life obstacles so that we can identify what is holding us back and what is going to help us to achieve our goals.

The grid highlights which areas are helpful to focus on. While they may all be relevant to some extent there is often just one or two areas that are relevant at any given time. The block becomes clear and with that clarity, the actions to address it are more obvious or accessible.

Each section of the grid can be an area that holds you back or helps you. For example, other people may not support you or be resistant to change, especially if they feel a change might impact them negatively. Others may have skills which are a resource you can use to help you, or they may have belief in you which helps build your own self-belief. If you believe in someone, they can believe in themselves. When you believe in yourself, anything is possible!

The nine major categories of life obstacles

Information or Knowledge Time	Skill	Self-Belief
Wellbeing	Other People	Time
Money	Fear	Motivation

Exercises

Think of an area that you are stuck on or struggling with. In this context, go through the nine different areas and give yourself a score of one (an area of total weakness) to ten (an area of strength).

The guide below which Michael Neill gives may help in this regard.

✧ You don't know what to do (Information).

✧ You know what to do, but you don't feel capable of doing it (Skill).

✧ You don't believe it can be done (Self-Belief).

✧ You don't have the energy or are too stressed out to do it (Wellbeing).

✧ Other people stand in your way (Other People).

✧ You don't have the time (Time).

✧ You don't have the money (Money).

✧ You're scared (Fear).

When you have identified the key areas that are holding you back, you can then ask yourself empowering questions around how to address it. For example:

✦ How can I ...?

✦ What do I need to do next?

✦ Who can I talk to?

✦ Who has that expertise?

✦ How can I capitalise or build on my strengths?

✦ How can I use my strengths to address the weakness?

✦ What needs to happen to increase my sense of ... wellbeing ... motivation ... self-belief?

When you have identified the areas of relevance, identify how you are going to use or leverage them. Allow them top up your reserves of energy and stamina so you persist.

To attain a balance in our thought process it is usually a case of highlighting and appreciating the 'good' rather than just addressing the 'bad' or the challenges.

✦ Think in terms of what characteristics or values you might need to progress. Pick just one you feel you need most at that time and let that be your guide. Some examples might be courage, creative thinking, confidence, patience, focus, decisiveness.

✦ You will know yourself what you need in any situation.

✦ Keep that word visible so that you see it frequently to remind you. Perhaps keep a picture message on your screensaver, or place a note on a mirror at home. Find an object which symbolises that quality or characteristic for you so that it becomes an affirmation that you can repeat throughout the day.

✦ In other areas of your day-to-day life, start to do and think in those terms. If, for example, you want to be more proactive you might book a check-up at the dentist when you don't actually have a toothache. You might suggest an outing rather than always going along with someone else's initiative. You could be the first to pick up the phone to resolve the issue with your sibling, friend or colleague. You could look at how you can do what you are doing differently, better, quicker. You could think in terms of action and doing rather than thinking and reflecting. The more you do this in ways that are easier or don't matter so much, the easier it is to do it in bigger situations when it matters a great deal.

✦ It does not mean that you have to change who you are. It just means you are not allowing some aspect to hold you back from what is important to you. It is like putting on a hard hat when you go on site, but it does not mean you have to wear it for the rest of your life.

Actions Speak Louder than Words

You can preach a better sermon with your life than with your lips.

Oliver Goldsmith

Is there something you have been talking about doing for ages but still haven't done? Most of us have a list of things we want to do but somehow don't seem to make the time for. Take a minute to think what your list might contain. Is it possible that talking about what you'd like to do lets you off the hook in terms of actually doing it? Or perhaps talking about it keeps it alive for you or in focus, giving you hope for the future?

Being aware of why we are talking about something and not doing it is important. Is it fear, lack of self-belief, lack of motivation, skills or knowledge, other people, time, money or our wellbeing?

Once we identify what is holding us back, we need to ask is it a reason or an excuse? Considering the questions on the following pages might help you clarify whether the reasons you give yourself are legitimate or whether they are ways of avoiding or 'excusing' yourself from whatever is necessary to realise your goals.

Exercises

What pay-off do you get by staying where you are?

We do things to gain pleasure or avoid pain, but we will do more to avoid the pain than to gain the pleasure. If I say I would love to be fit enough to see the view from the top of Mount Kilimanjaro but I'm not known for my sense of adventure, would I then tell myself that what I have to do to make this happen is more upsetting than the pleasure I think it will bring? While this is not exactly an everyday example, in life it is often the case that we are prompted to take action only when not doing something is a more upsetting prospect than doing it.

Why is doing it important? What feelings do you think it will bring? What values will it fill? How will you feel when you have done it?

Based on the above example, complete one of the sentences below and keep going until you cannot find another reason:

I want it because _____

Or

I want to do it because _____

What is stopping you? What has to change to move it forward?

What are you waiting for?

Does the way you treat your loved ones contradict your feelings for them?

Our actions become our behaviour, character and reputation. They create the experience other people have of us. If I say I love you but on a day-to-day basis do not treat you with love and respect, how are you going to feel? Loved or disrespected? Accepted or judged? Connected or rejected?

As the poet Maya Angelou said 'people will forget what you said, people will forget what you did, but people will never forget how you made them feel'.

So is there anyone in your life whom you say you love but to whom you may not be demonstrating it on a daily basis?

Do you need to be honest with yourself?

What example are you setting for those around you?

If you are a parent this is an easy one to identify with. We are often so busy telling our children what to do and not do and trying to pass on our values that we forget to check in on the example we are setting. We tell them that honesty is the best policy, but do we spin a few white lies during the day? We tell them that they should be kind with their words and yet they may overhear us being anything but. We want them to listen to us but are we really listening to them?

In a work situation, anyone in a leadership position has an important influence. Consistently, those who are authentic command the most respect. Leadership demands diverse organisational and strategic skills, but you can only be a leader if you have followers and people will only follow those who are authentic.

Be positive. Be kind and caring. Challenge yourself. Believe in yourself. Laugh. Let your actions speak for themselves. Allow yourself to lean towards those who inspire you.

What you do speaks so loudly that I cannot hear what you say.

Ralph Waldo Emerson

Colour Blind

The best colour in the whole world is the one that looks good on you.

Coco Chanel

Have you ever been struck by the fact that bargain prices and special offers in shops are so often printed on a red or yellow background? That is no accident. The business world and marketing companies have known for a long time the importance and power of colour in branding and packaging.

Pharmaceutical companies know the importance of the psychology of colour when it comes to medication. From Egyptian times, pills were round and white, but from the mid-twentieth century colour came into play. Cultural differences may apply but generally red is synonymous with speed and prowess while blue suggests relaxation or calm.

We are blessed to have a broad spectrum of colour all around us. We have it for a reason. If colour were not so important we could happily live our lives in black and white. But it is there and each colour can have a different impact on how we feel, the choices and decisions we make and the quality of our life and experiences.

Colour can raise our blood pressure, stimulate our appetite, and soothe our eyes and our soul. The hues on everything around us are in a state of flux, continuously altered by sunrises, sunsets and the ever-changing seasons and light. Colour can be linked with musical notes, countries and cultures, interior design and much, much more. So how can we start to use colour to enhance our day-to-day experience and impact how we are feeling, how others perceive us, and improve the quality of our lives?

Exercises

Have a look at your home environment.

✧ Which colours feature in the rooms?

✧ What does your environment say about you?

✧ What do you want it to say?

✧ What do you need in your life right now?

✧ What impact do the colours already there have and are they what you want and need either for you or that particular room? For example, yellow in the kitchen can stimulate your appetite but yellow in the bedroom (if overused) may not be conducive to restful sleep.

✧ What colour would you like to introduce?

✧ It does not have to mean a repaint. It could be a cushion, bunch of flowers or bowl of apples.

Have a look at your wardrobe.

✧ If you stand back and look objectively, does your wardrobe represent the colour spectrum?

✧ Is one colour featured more than others?

✧ If you find your wardrobe features a lot of dark or similar colours, consider introducing some variety: red is very much associated with power, energy and confidence; yellow will lift your spirits; pink is the colour of love for yourself and of healing; blue is for integrity, loyalty and communication; green is for balance and growth; brown is down to earth; grey is for compromise; orange is for optimism and vitality with endurance.

Have a look around you:

✧ As you make your way through the day look around you with fresh eyes.

✧ Notice the colour in everything around you.

✧ Notice the play of light on things and how that can change the hue.

Have a look at what you eat:

✧ What colour do you need to introduce to rebalance? And how can you do this? The foods you eat can matter: yellow and orange can lift your mood, so oranges and pineapples are a wonderful pick-me-up.

Car manufacturer Henry Ford once famously stated that customers could choose a car in any colour as long as it was black. However, we have a glorious spectrum of colours available and our lives can be so enriched when we use them.

Hugging Your Way to Good Health

A hug is like a boomerang – you get it back right away.

Family Circus, Bil Keane

Some people are natural huggers and some are not. If you are not, you may dread those who seem to be totally oblivious to that fact as they lunge towards you for a hearty embrace. Why on earth would someone want to greet you with a squeeze? Your natural preference apart, consider the benefits of a hug.

Hugging (and anything which produces warm feelings, emotional contact and emotion) is good for your health as it produces oxytocin which is also referred to as the love or trust hormone. It is believed to lower the risk of heart disease, reduce stress, boost your immune system, ease depression and much more besides.

Hugging relaxes muscles and eases tension (when you get over being self-conscious about it). It enhances relationships and underscores connection. It makes us feel good. And the best thing about it is that you are giving and receiving at the same time … even with a reluctant hugger!

Virginia Satir, a respected family therapist, suggests:

We need four hugs a day for survival. We need eight hugs
a day for maintenance. We need twelve hugs a day for
growth.

Paul Zak, a renowned neuroeconomist, refers to oxytocin as the 'moral molecule' and he recommends eight hugs a day for a better world. If you have not got a ready-made family of fellow huggers, you may wonder how one achieves that. Hug a pillow, wrap your arms around yourself and give yourself a huge hug. You may have to start by being the one to 'give' the hug and others just get used to you and allow themselves to hug you back.

If you have a family, children often take the lead. There is good morning, goodbye leaving for work or school, hello again coming home, goodnight, well done, love you, thank you for helping and whatever else comes to mind. When with friends, take the initiative to hug. A warm smile, embrace and heartfelt greeting create a sense of wellbeing in both parties. If you feel uncomfortable saying I love you, find the words that allow you to express how you feel about someone on a more regular basis. Love you lots, love meeting up with you, really enjoy our time together … whatever allows you to acknowledge the connection and bond.

As previously mentioned, anything that produces warm feelings and contact produces oxytocin. Besides hugging, some other ways to produce it are:

✦ Acts of kindness and compassion. With an act of kindness, you feel good, the person receiving it feels good and anyone who observes it feels good.

✦ Love: if you love someone you will feel warmly about them and this will be reciprocated.

✦ Being quick to forgive and letting those close to you know that you don't nurse grudges.

Exercises

So, to boost your oxytocin levels and sense of well-being:

✦ If you are someone who is not naturally comfortable hugging, perhaps take the time to find out more about the vast array of benefits for mind, body and soul that we get from hugging, love and kindness. This can help to tip the scales between feeling uncomfortable and being prepared to stretch the comfort zone to avail of the benefits.

✦ Look for and avail of opportunities to give and receive hugs – the longer the better. Let them show what words might not be able to say. Let them connect you with others and enhance relationships. Let them bring support and comfort and acceptance and joy.

✦ Hug wholeheartedly … be present when you are present.

✦ Look for opportunities to perform random acts of kindness. They are like virtual hugs. Pay the toll for the person behind you. Offer someone your umbrella if they have none. Take the time to answer the survey questions for the person who is struggling to get someone's time or attention. If you are buying a cup of coffee, pay for another cup and tell them to offer it to the next person who comes along. Offer to do a school run, offer help to a colleague in work, give someone your time … it is often the most precious gift we can give … Let someone go ahead of you in a queue.

Sometimes we don't need advice or therapy, we just need a hug. Sometimes we may not know what to say to someone or what to do to help, and they may just need a hug.

Adding Life to Your Years

Improving your life doesn't have to be about changing
everything – it's about making changes that count.

Oprah Winfrey

There are times in our lives when we really notice and appreciate where we are, what we are doing, or who we are with. There are times when we feel happy and content. There are times when we are living our lives to the full. And then there are many times when the opposite is the case.

If we are coasting by on auto pilot we may feel like victims of circumstance or powerless in relation to the quality of the life we are living. Life can throw us a curveball which focuses our minds: perhaps you or someone you know is diagnosed with a serious illness; perhaps you lose your job or your home; perhaps you lose a friendship. I have often heard people speak about how a neighbour may have extended their home, blocking a view they always enjoyed. Previously, they may have been so busy in their mind and day-to-day life that they didn't 'see' the view every day, but knowing it is going or gone upsets them greatly. They no longer have the option to see it if they want.

They say that we often only really appreciate something when it is gone. In terms of this book we are talking about our lives and that does not seem like a good approach …

There is an amazing poem called 'The Dash' by Linda Ellis which highlights that at the end of our life the date of our birth and death is often shown with a dash in-between. She challenges/ encourages us to make our dash count. Regardless of the dates and time in between we can make the most of that time.

We have varying levels of control over the quantity of our life (some elements are within our control with regard to how we look after our body, lifestyle, etc. but there is a lot outside of it). We do, however, have a lot more control over the quality than we may have thought.

As mentioned earlier in the book, there is a great saying that we should enjoy the little things in life because one day we will look back and realise that they were big things. When we think in terms of improving the quality of our life and our day-to-day experiences, the same applies. The little things we do today can lead to big changes. Each section in this book suggests ways in which we can improve that quality. Either separately or combined they work if you apply them but they are just some suggestions and there are many more.

Exercises

In relation to the quality of your life, think in terms of a scale of one to ten.

✦ What would a ten be?

✦ You need to be specific here as most people don't know what they want but are sure they don't have it. Knowing what a ten looks like is half the battle!

✦ How would you rate your life at the moment? This is your assessment of the quality, not someone else's.

✦ If the number is low and your energy is low around the situation in general, think in terms of why there is hope … there is always hope; sometimes that can be as simple as acknowledging the fact as that you are alive, so where there is life there is hope. Using this as a starting point can help shift your thinking around the situation, which in turn changes your emotions around it, which can free up the energy, initiative or inspiration to improve it.

✦ What would have to change to bring it up on the scale to the next level/number?

✦ Which of the exercises helped or can help? Commit to consciously applying it until it becomes your natural way of being in the world.

✦ Think of two or three other things which could help improve the quality of life in general. You will know best what you need right now. Discover and design your own.

✦ Share them with a friend or colleague, and in doing so it will reinforce it for you and spread some positive and empowering resources for others.

Adding life to our years is about deciding to improve the quality of the life and years that we have. The alternative involves sitting in the passenger seat of life, having no control over the journey. It is not making our dash count. The best time to start improving the quality of the present and of the years ahead is now. Today. It is all we have and are sure of, so make it count. Decide today to add life to your years.